Visiting the Chiropractor

A Social Story

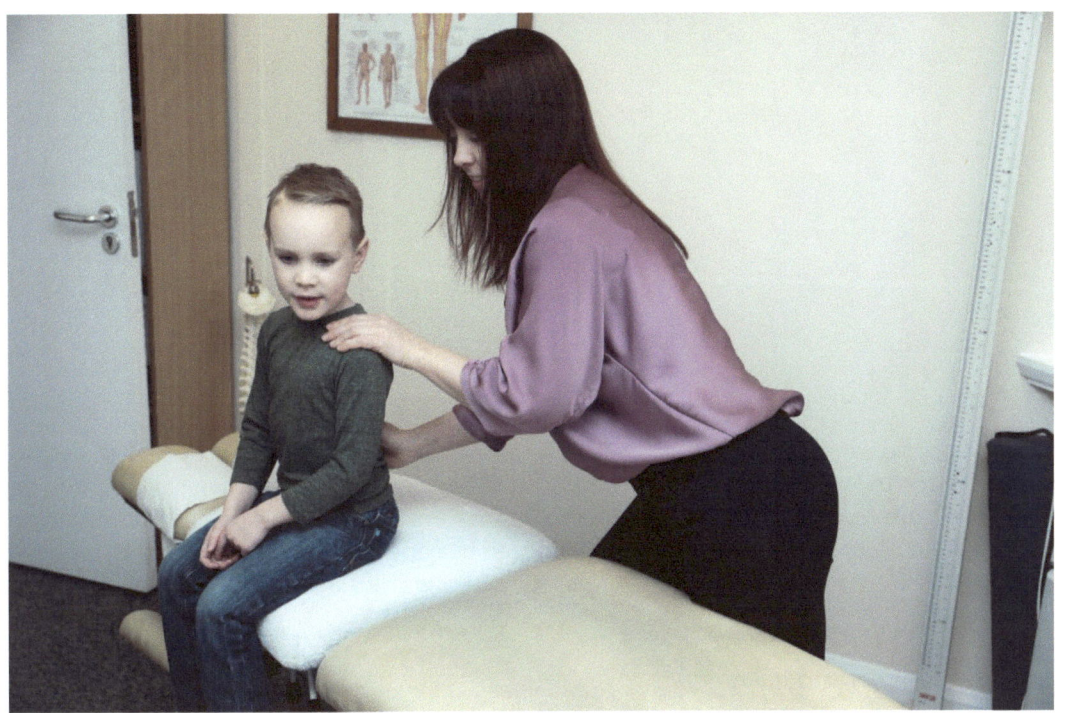

Samantha Kingdon, DC

Jennie Lynn Gillham

Copyright © 2018 by Jennie Lynn Gillham.

All rights reserved. No part of this publication may be reproduced, distributed or transmitted in any form or by any means, including photocopying, recording, or other electronic or mechanical methods, without the prior written permission of the publisher, except in the case of brief quotations embodied in critical reviews and certain other noncommercial uses permitted by copyright law. For permission requests, email courageouschiropractor@gmail.com addressed "Attention: Social Story Publisher."

Published by Phoenix Cry Publishing, LLC

www.CourageousChiropractor.com/

Book design © 2017, BookDesignTemplates.com

Photography: Erica Lindsey Photography www.ericalindseyphtography.com/

Editor: Lindsey Marcus

Ordering Information: Special discounts are available on quantity purchases by chiropractors, corporations, associations, and others. For details, contact courageouschiropractor@gmail.com

First Edition

Print Edition ISBN 978-0-9995191-2-7

Dedicated to Brayden and Jenn Ghigna

Special thanks to our photographer, Erica Lindsey

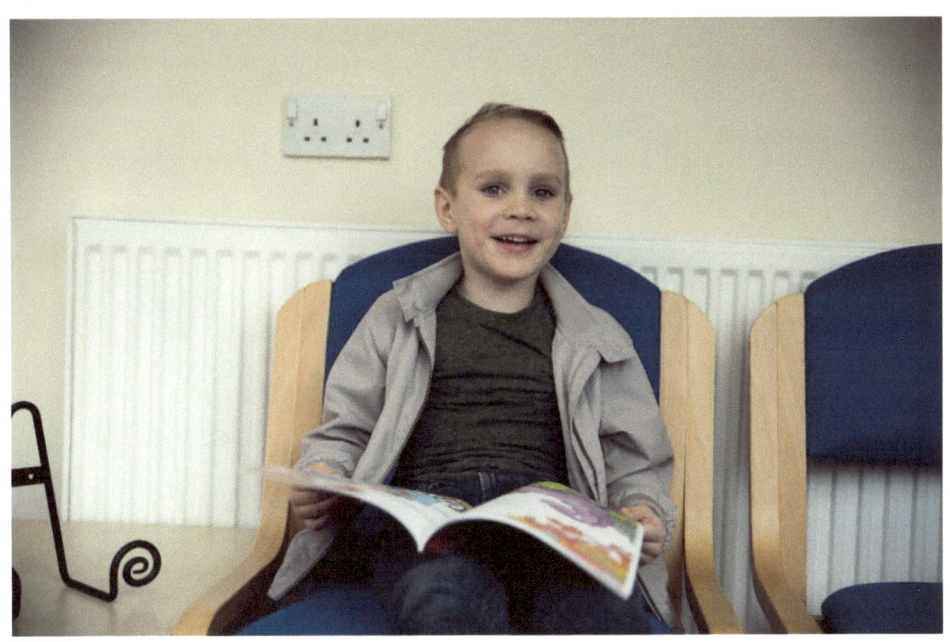

Meet Brayden. Brayden has autism. Part of his routine care is visiting the chiropractor.

Brayden let the photographer take the pictures in this book so other kids could read about what it is like visiting the chiropractor.

This book is dedicated to him and his mother, Jenn, an amazing advocate for special needs families.

I go to the chiropractor.

Once I am at the office, I can read a book or play with a toy.

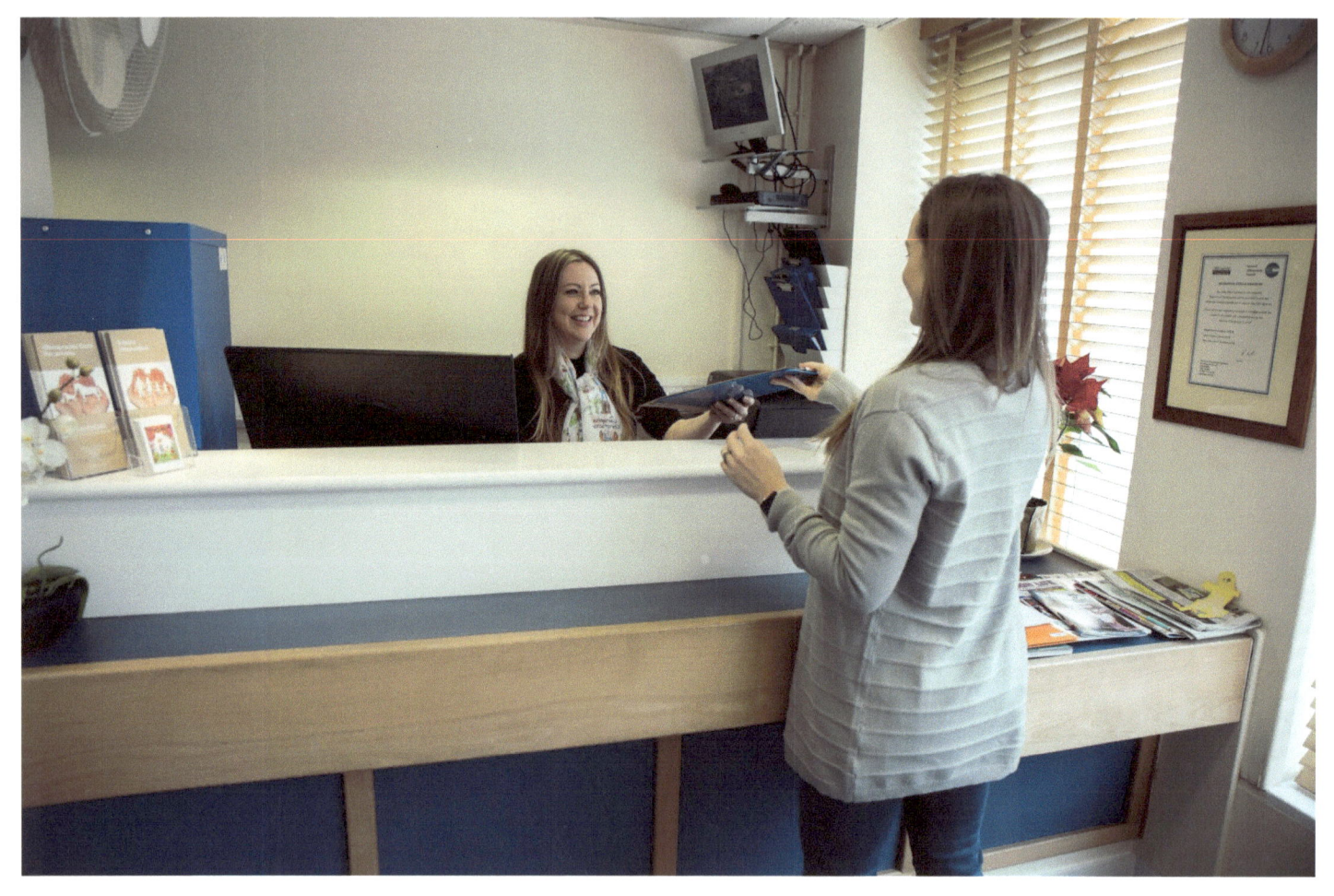

Mom tells the person at the front desk we are here.

The chiropractor comes out to meet me. She tells me her name is Miss Sam.

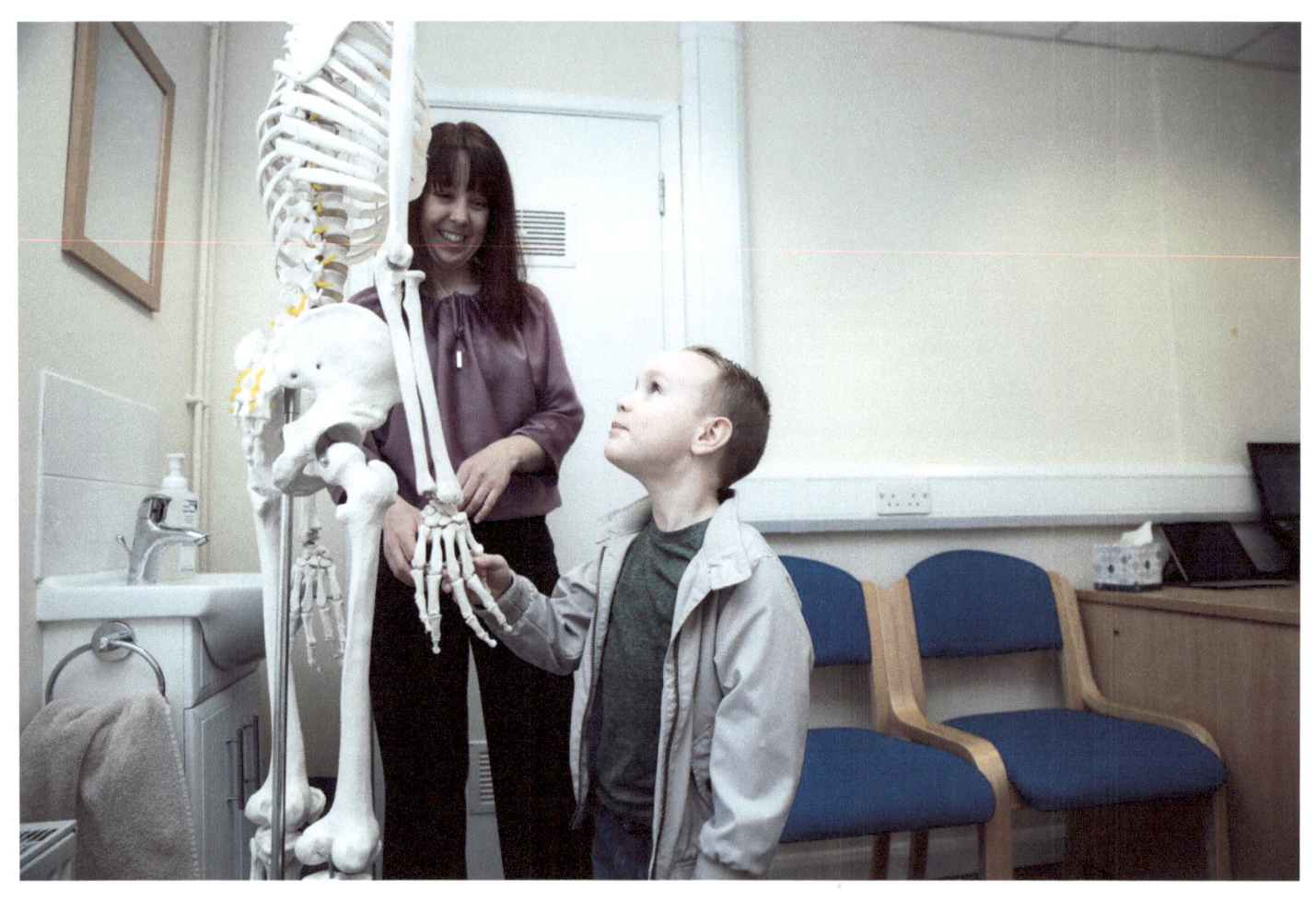

Mom and I follow Miss Sam. Miss Sam shows me her room.

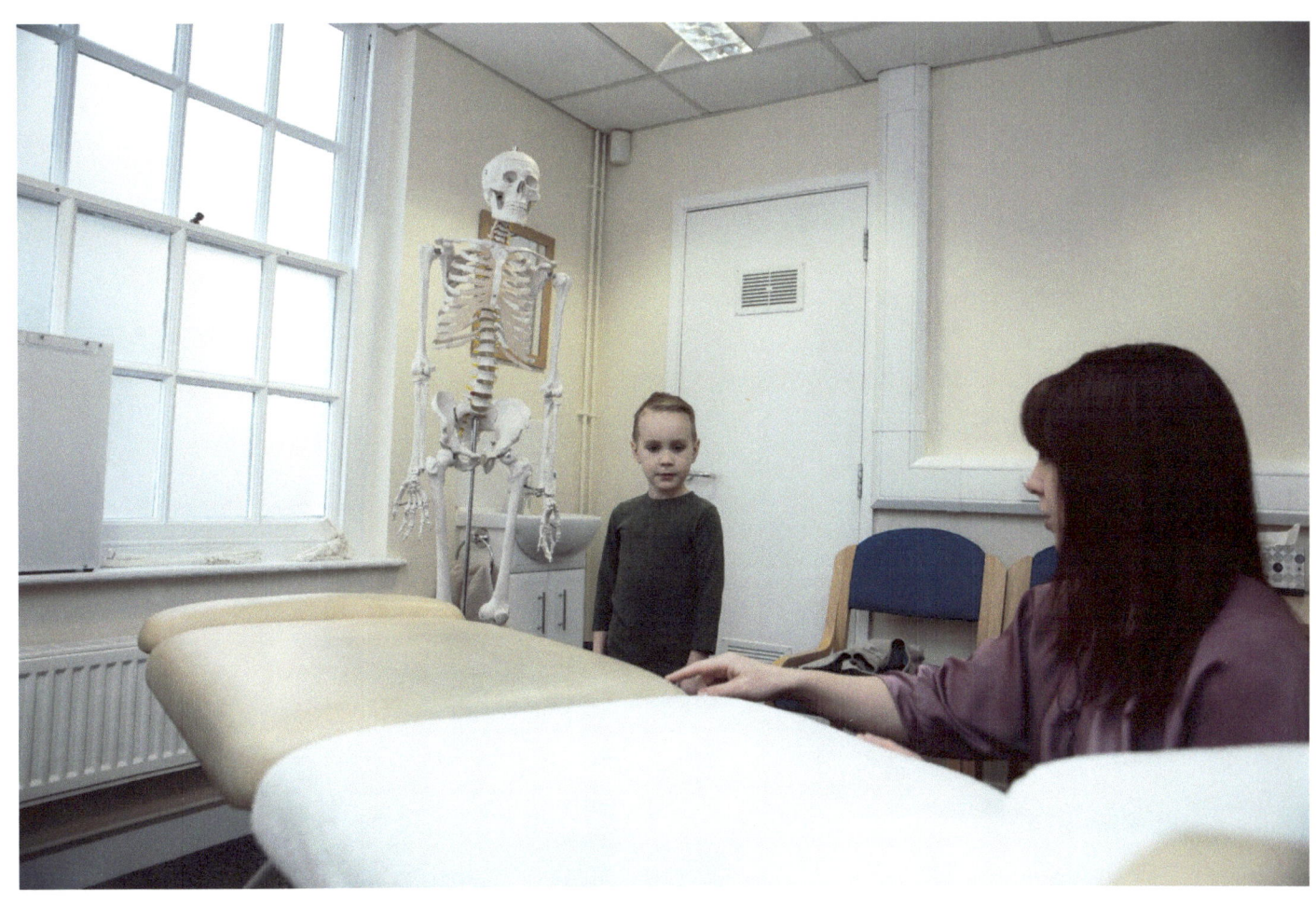

She shows me the table that moves.

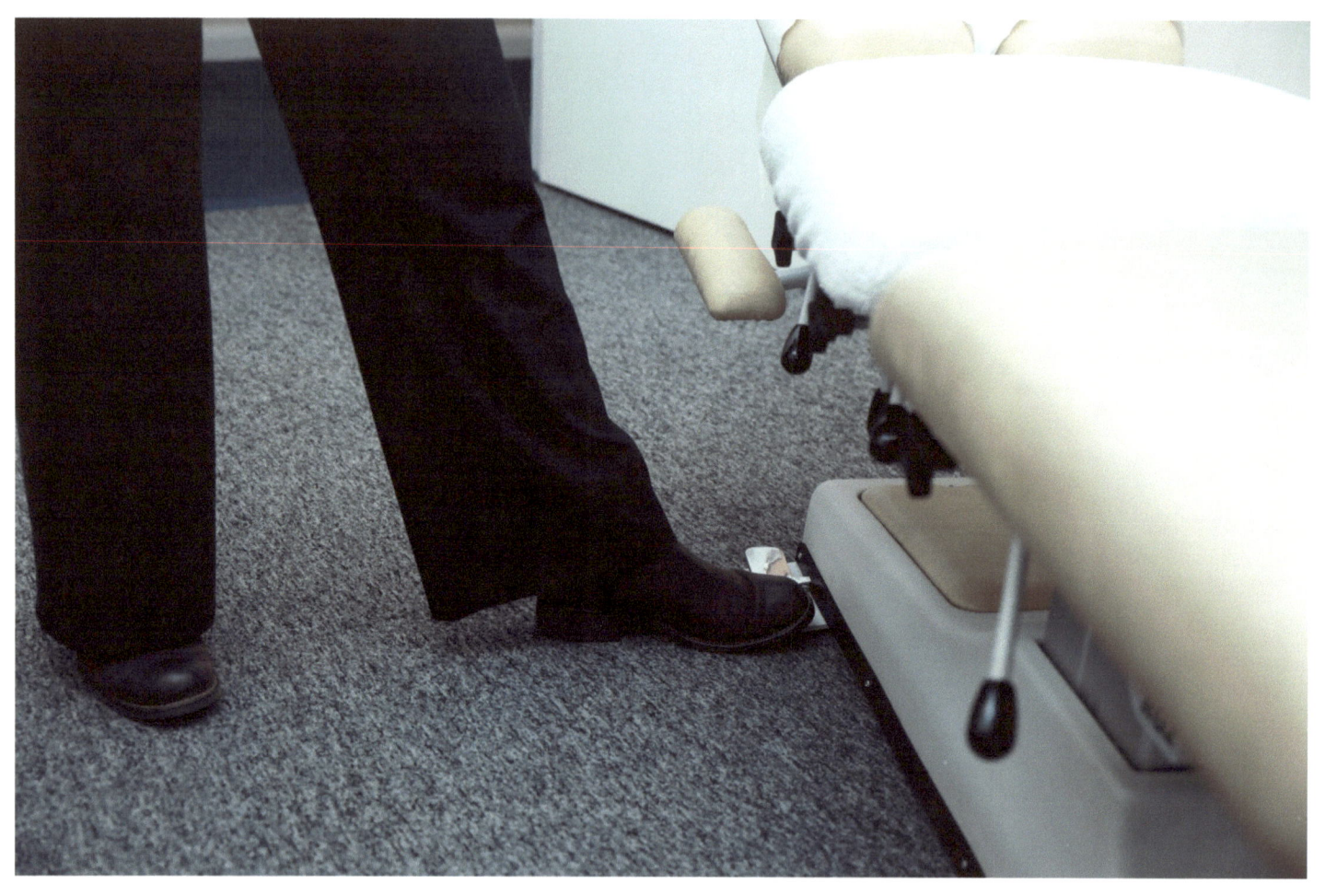

The table makes lots of noisy sounds. The table goes up and down.

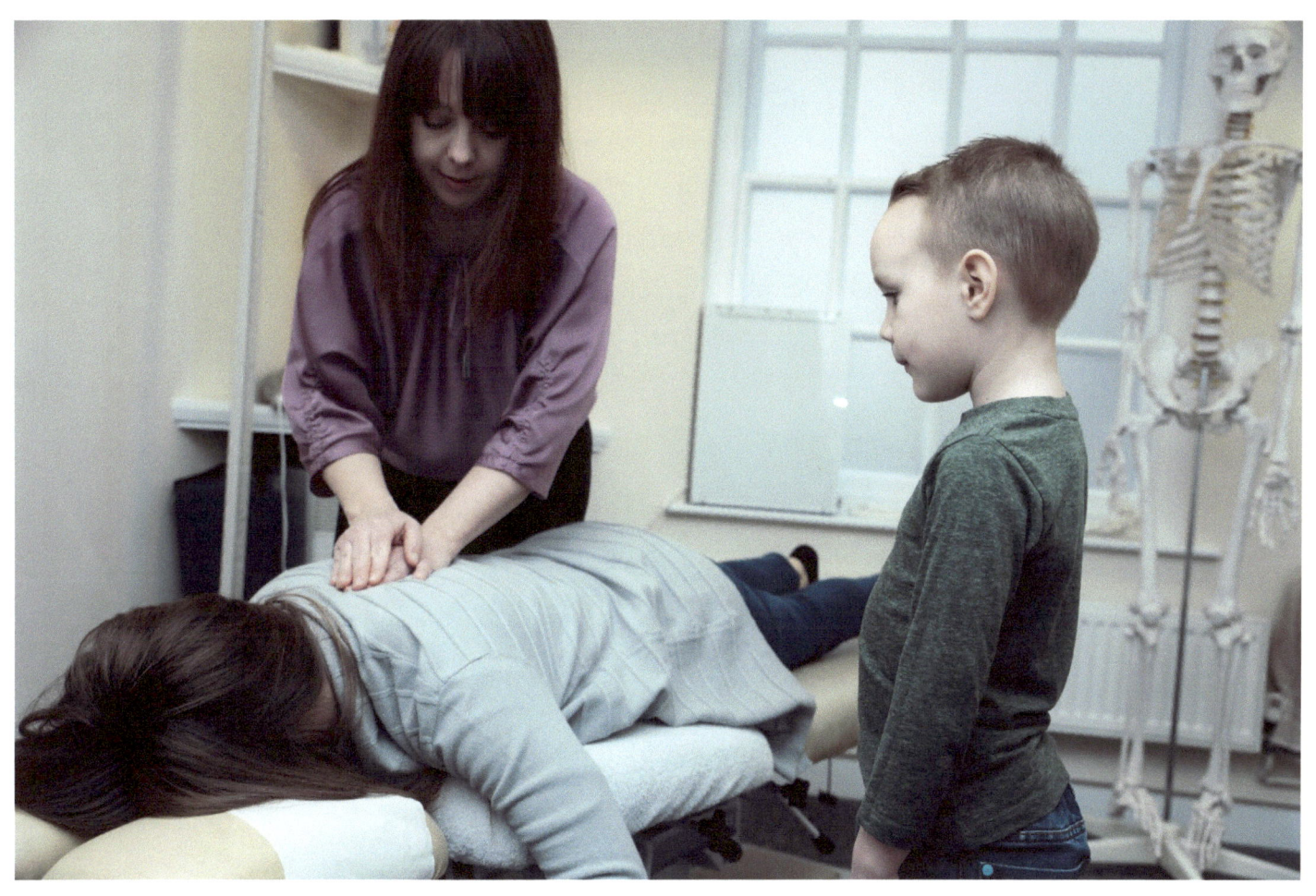

Mom rests on the table.

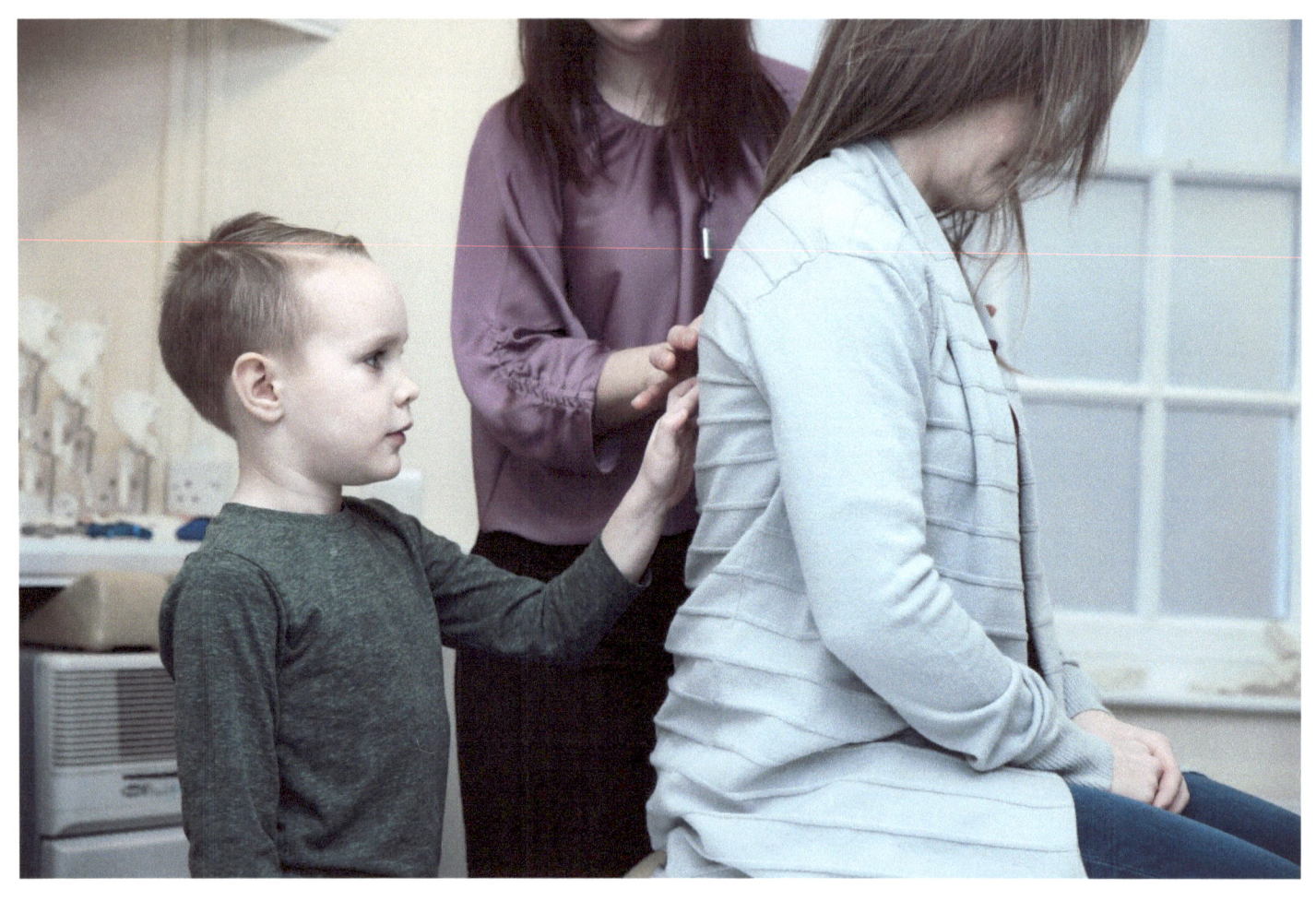

I help Miss Sam work on Mom to learn about what will be done to me.

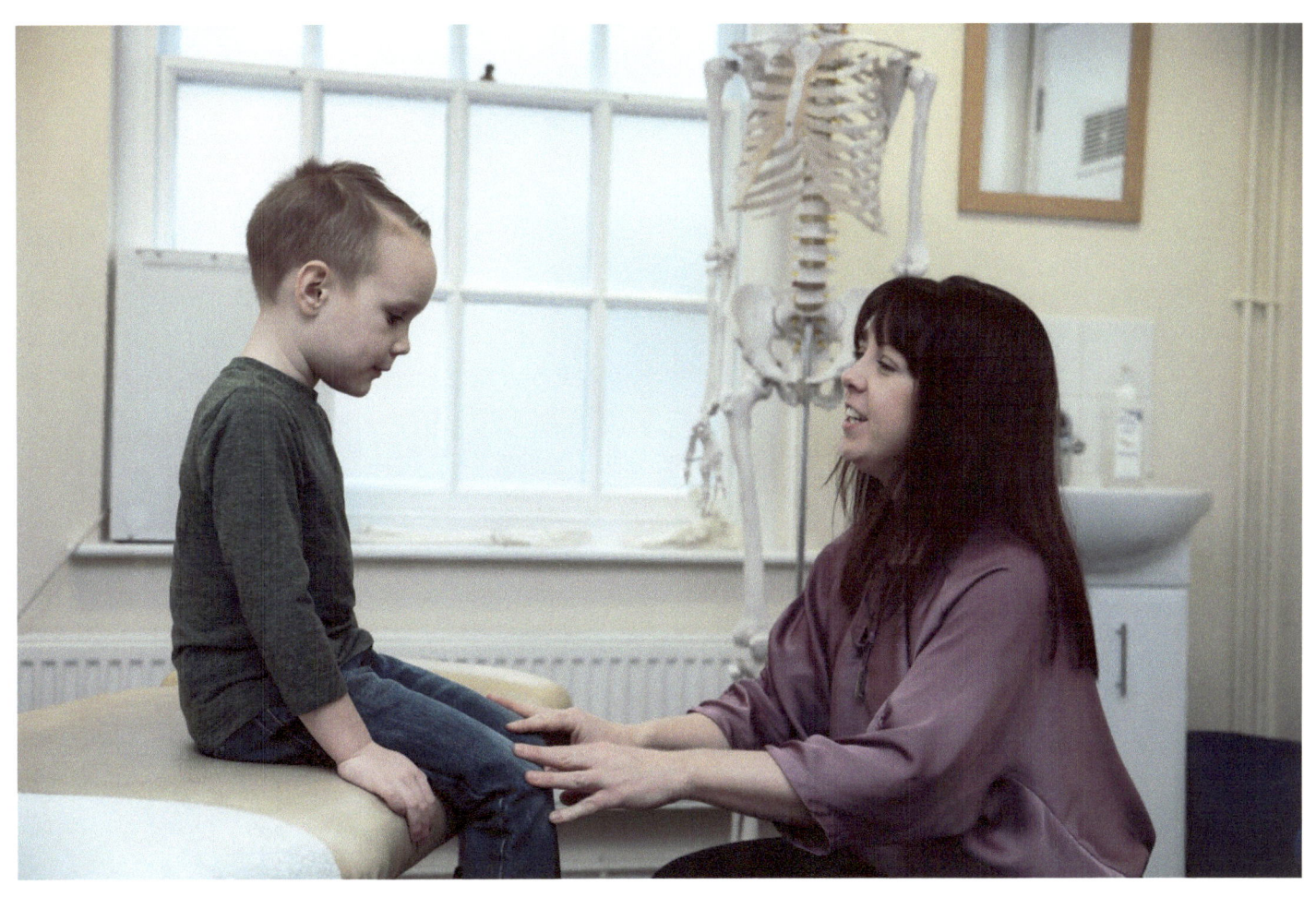

Now it is my turn to sit on the table.

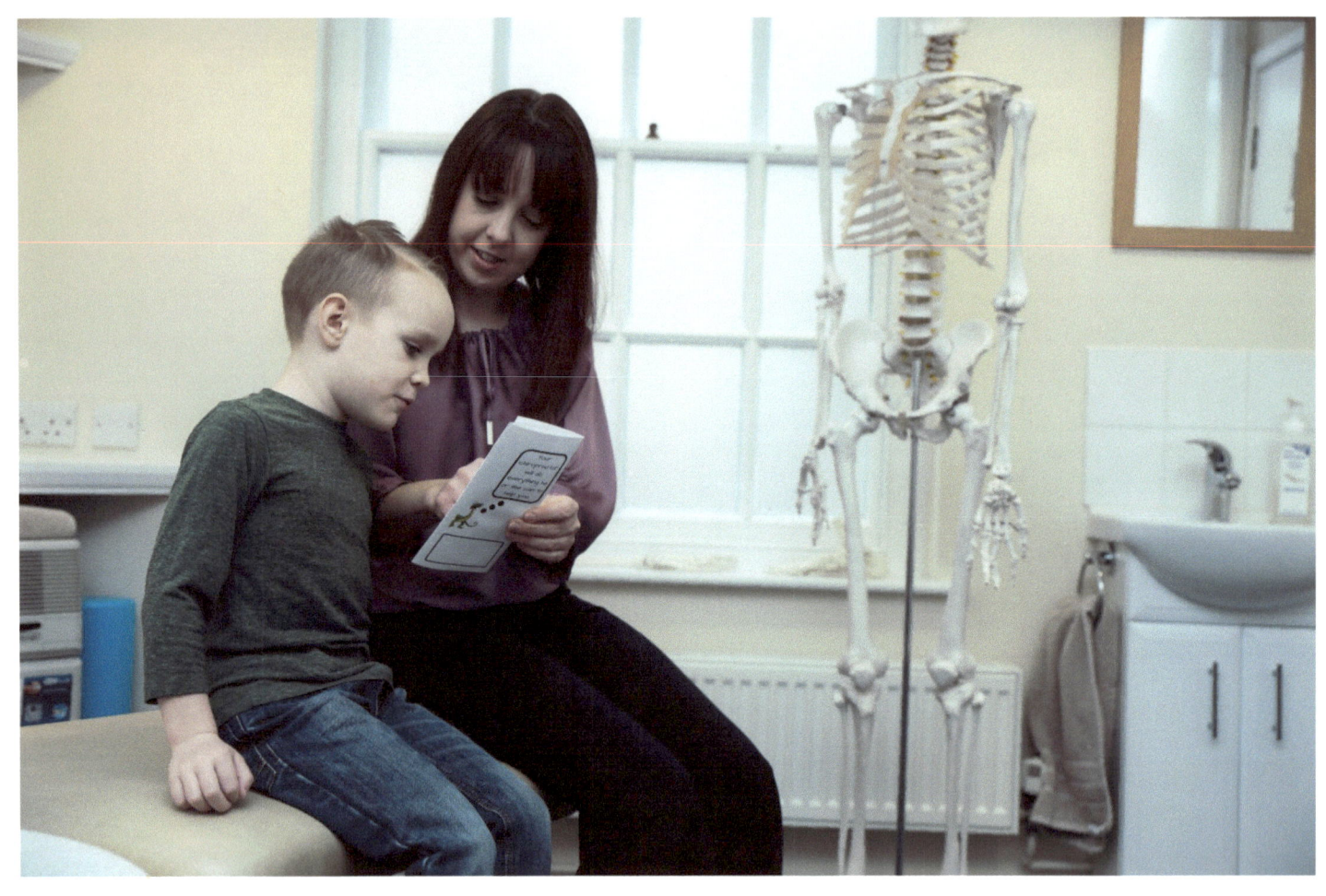

Miss Sam talks with me about anything that hurts.

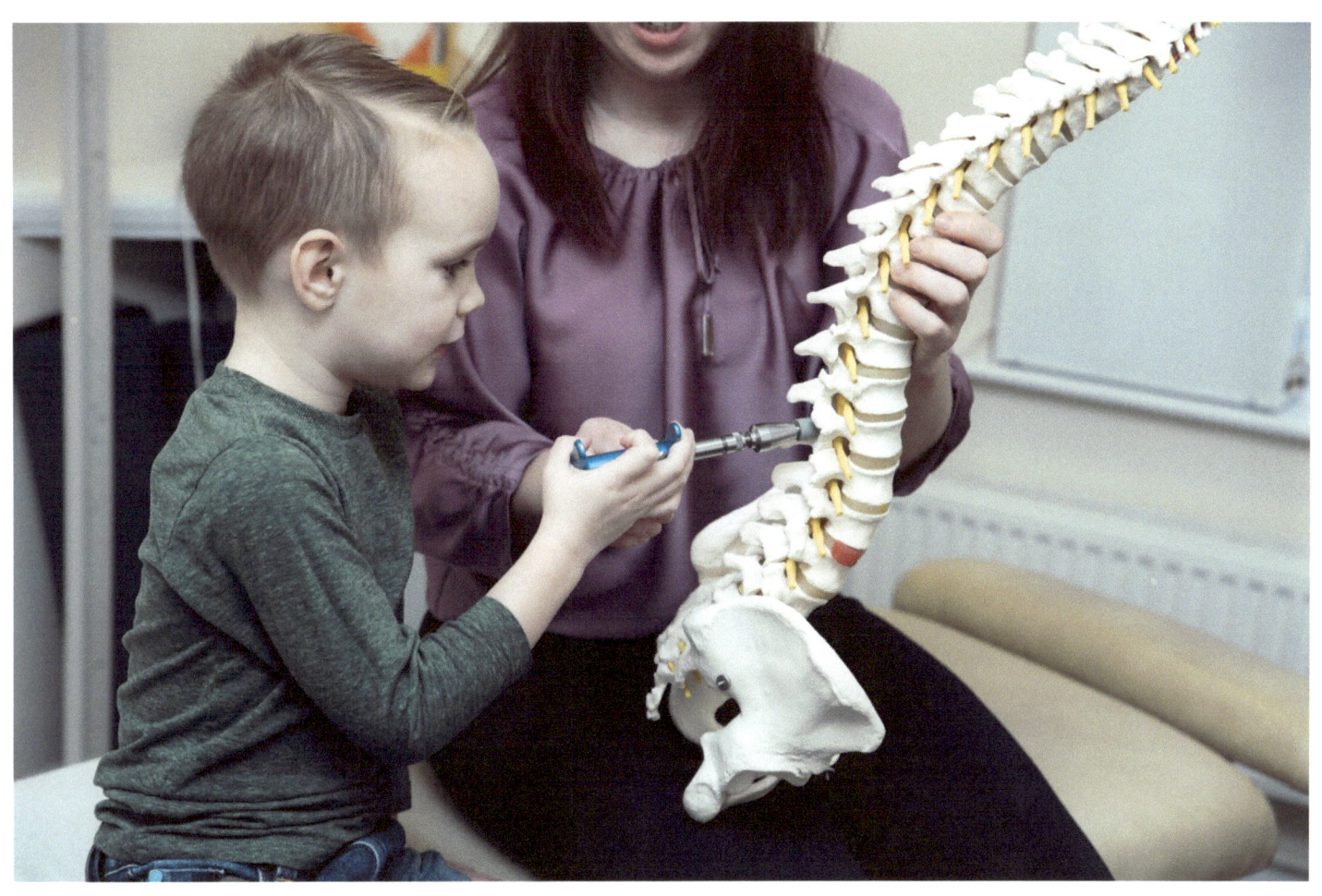

Miss Sam shows me a tool called an adjuster.

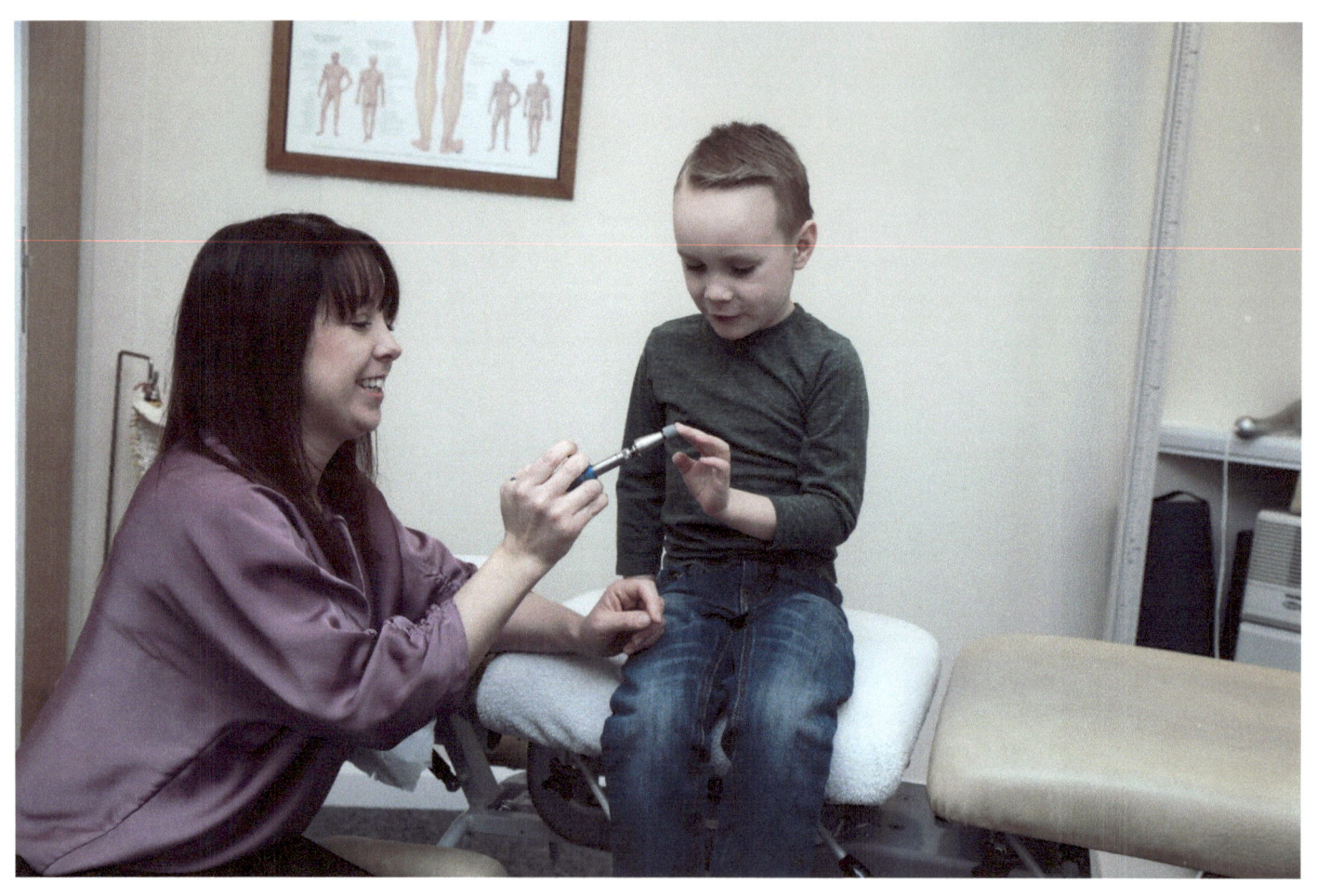

Miss Sam uses the adjuster on my finger so I know it does not hurt.

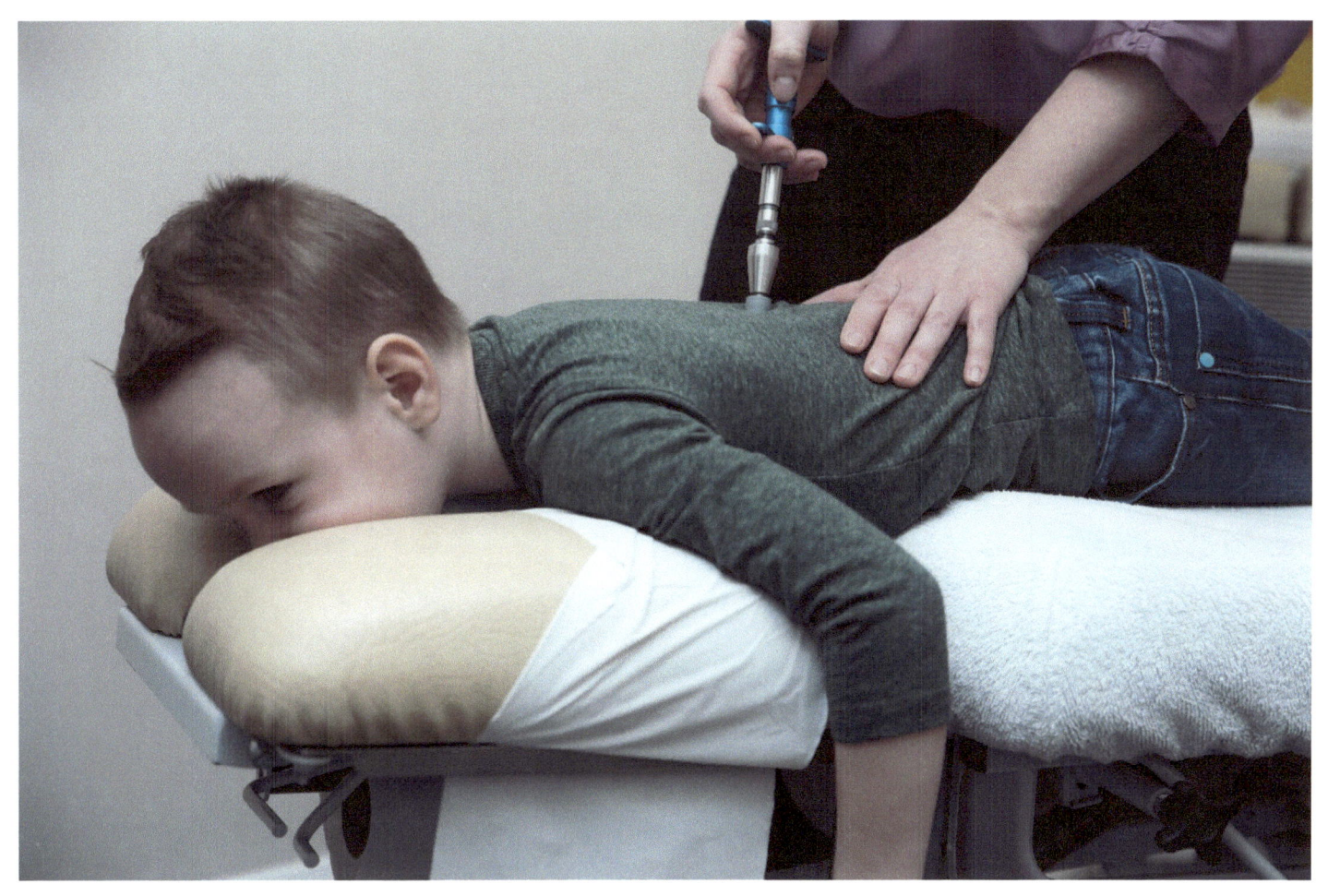

Miss Sam uses the adjuster on me.

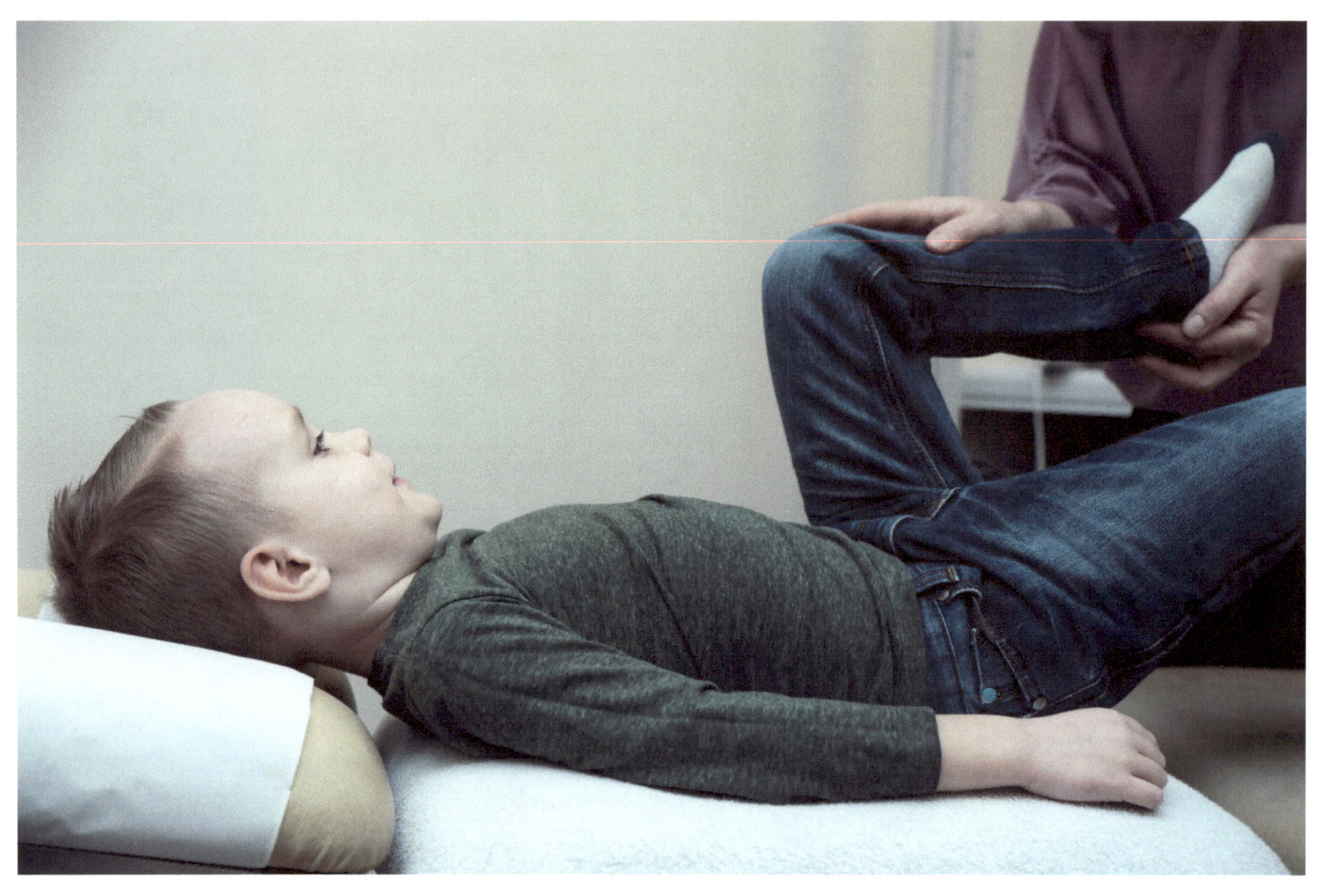

Miss Sam uses her hands. Sometimes I lie on my back.

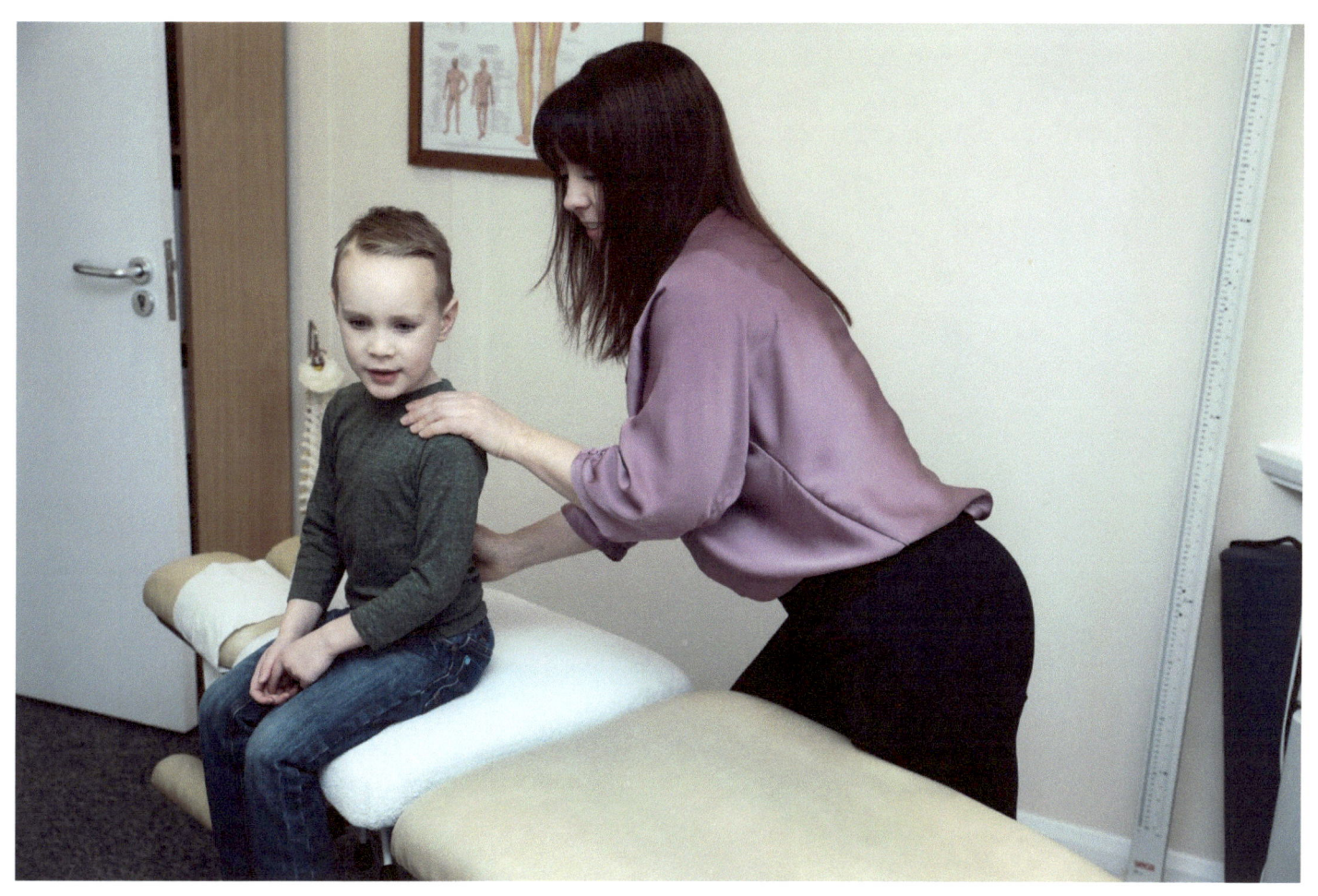

Sometimes I sit up.

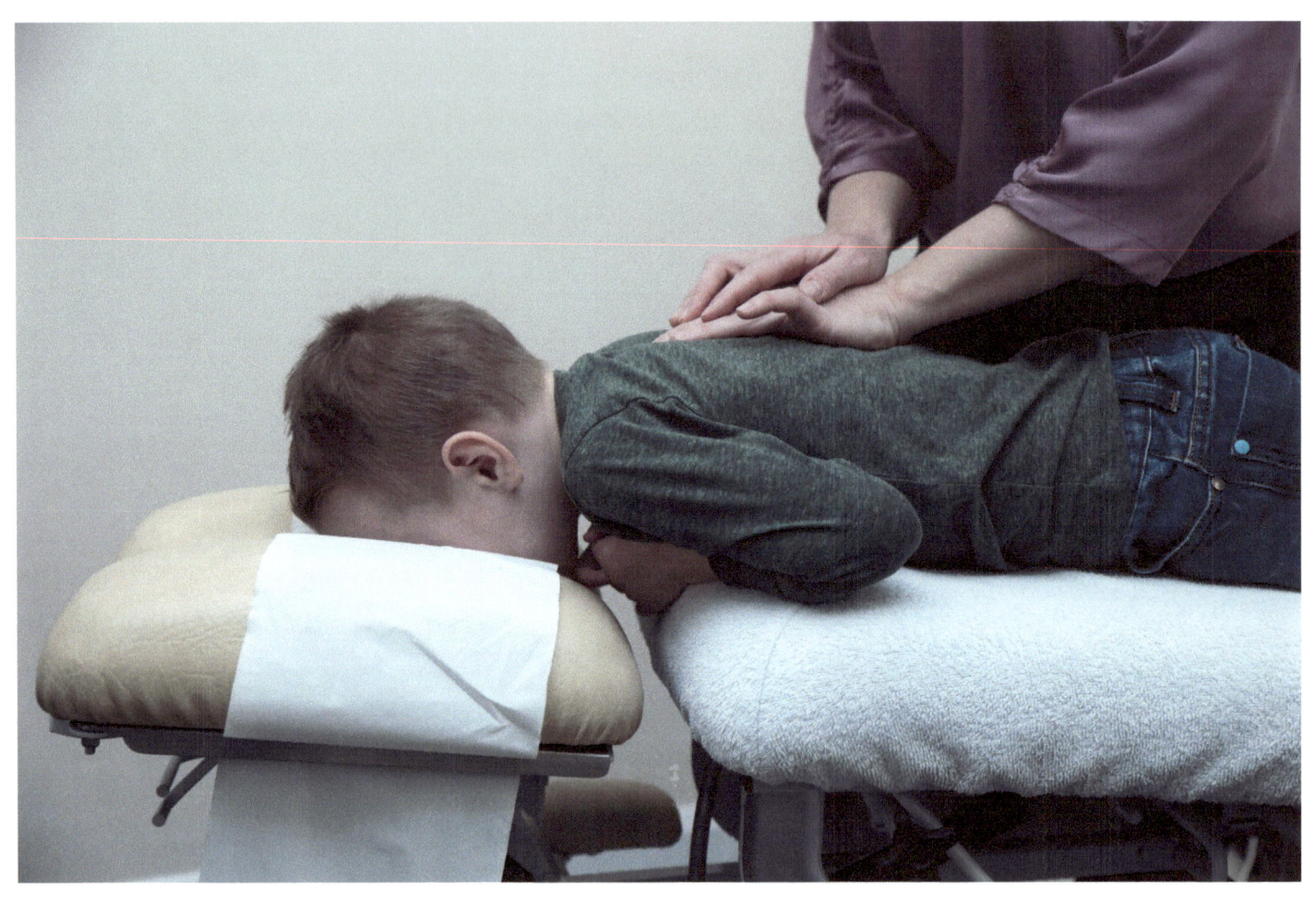

Sometimes I am on my stomach.

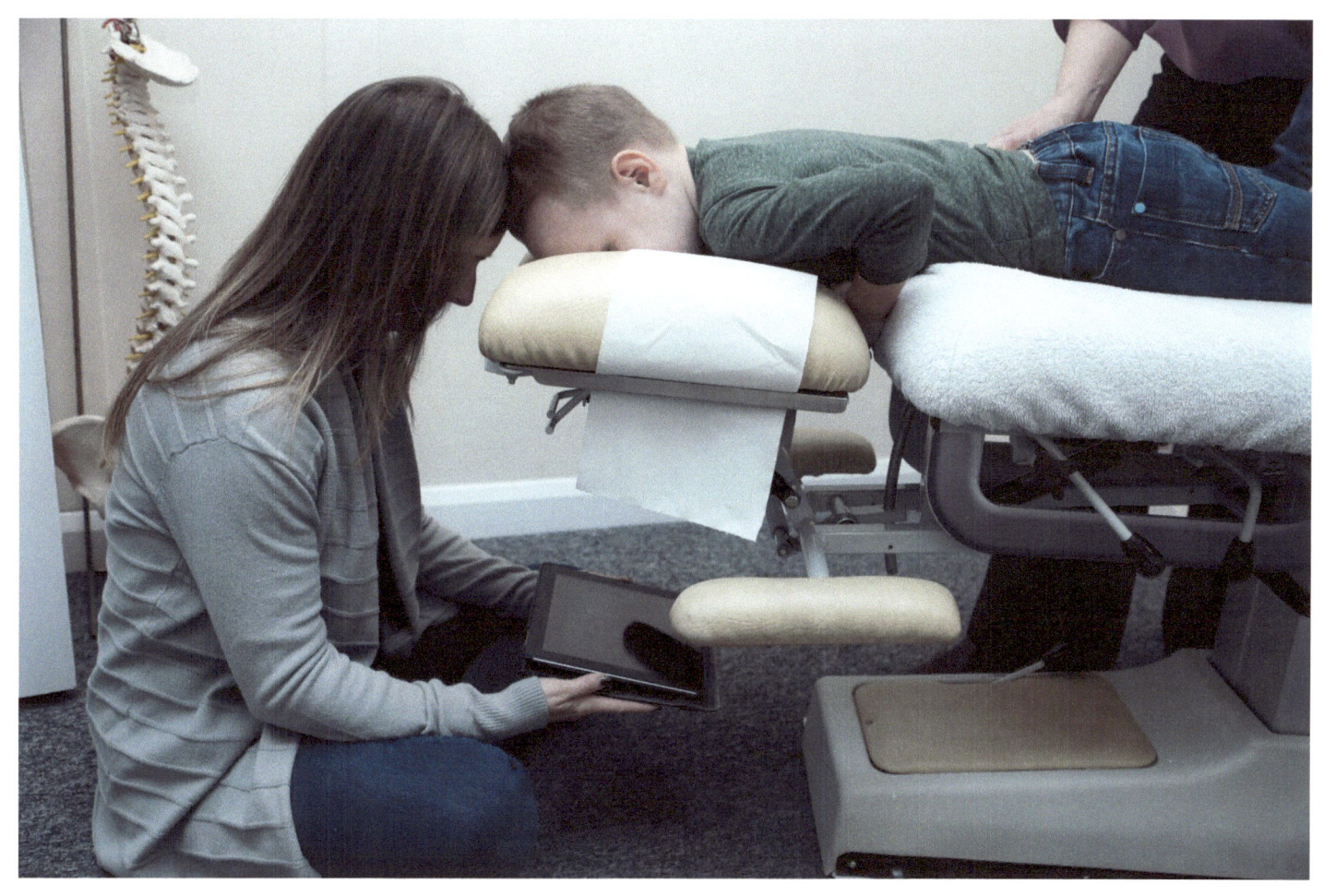

Sometimes Mom lets me watch a show on the tablet through the hole in the pillow to help me relax.

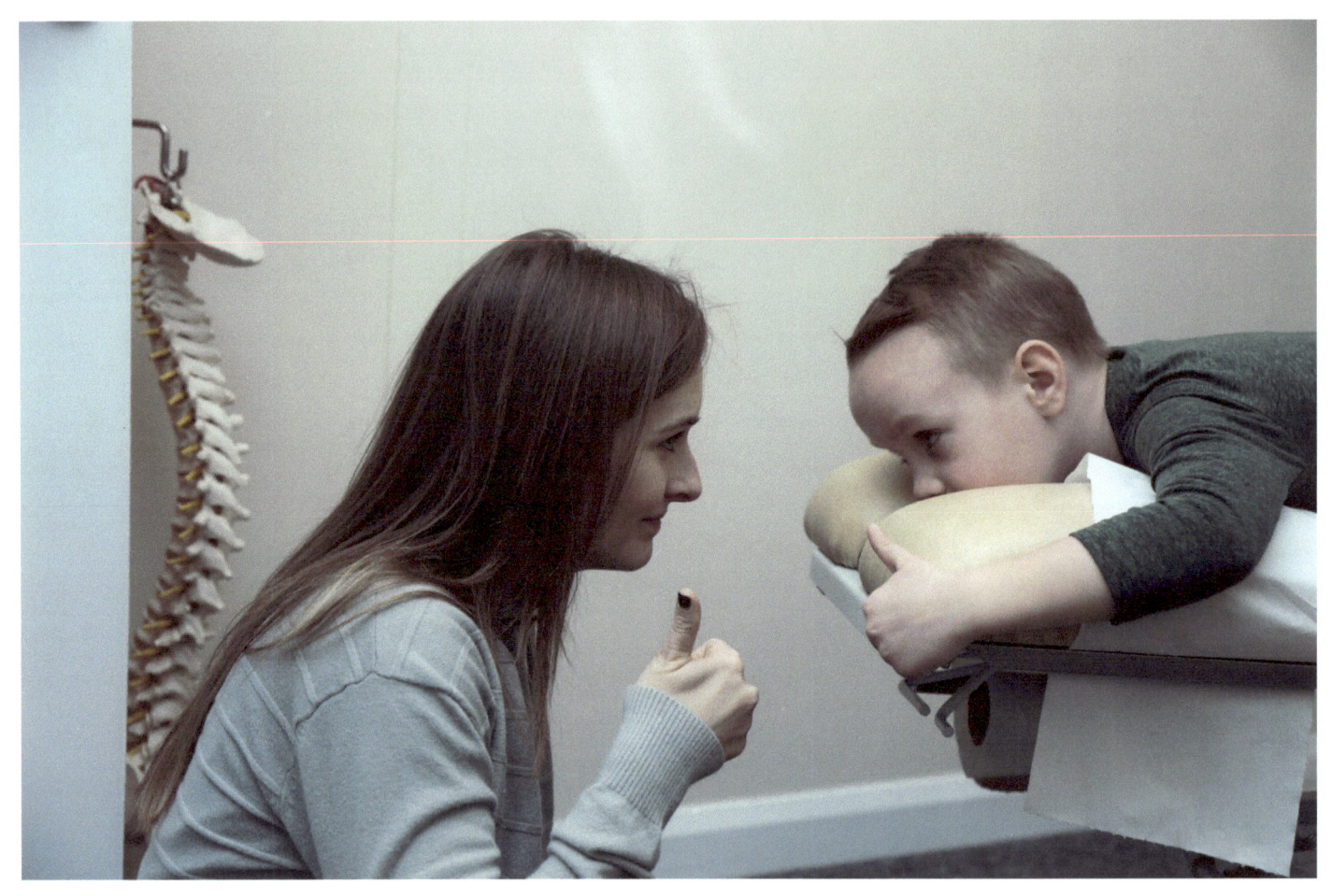

Mom asks me how I'm doing. I give her a thumbs up.

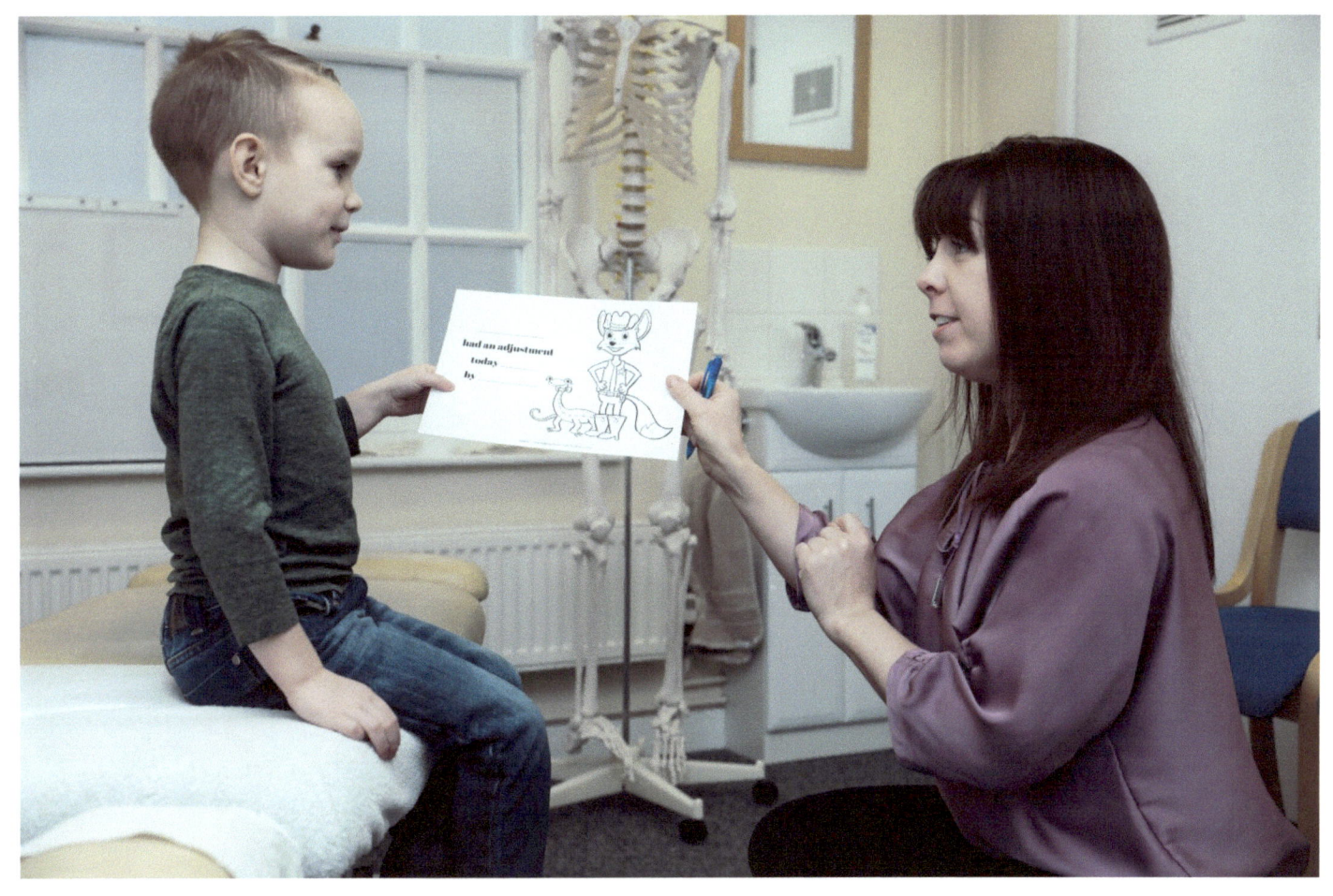

When I am done, Miss Sam gives me a certificate.

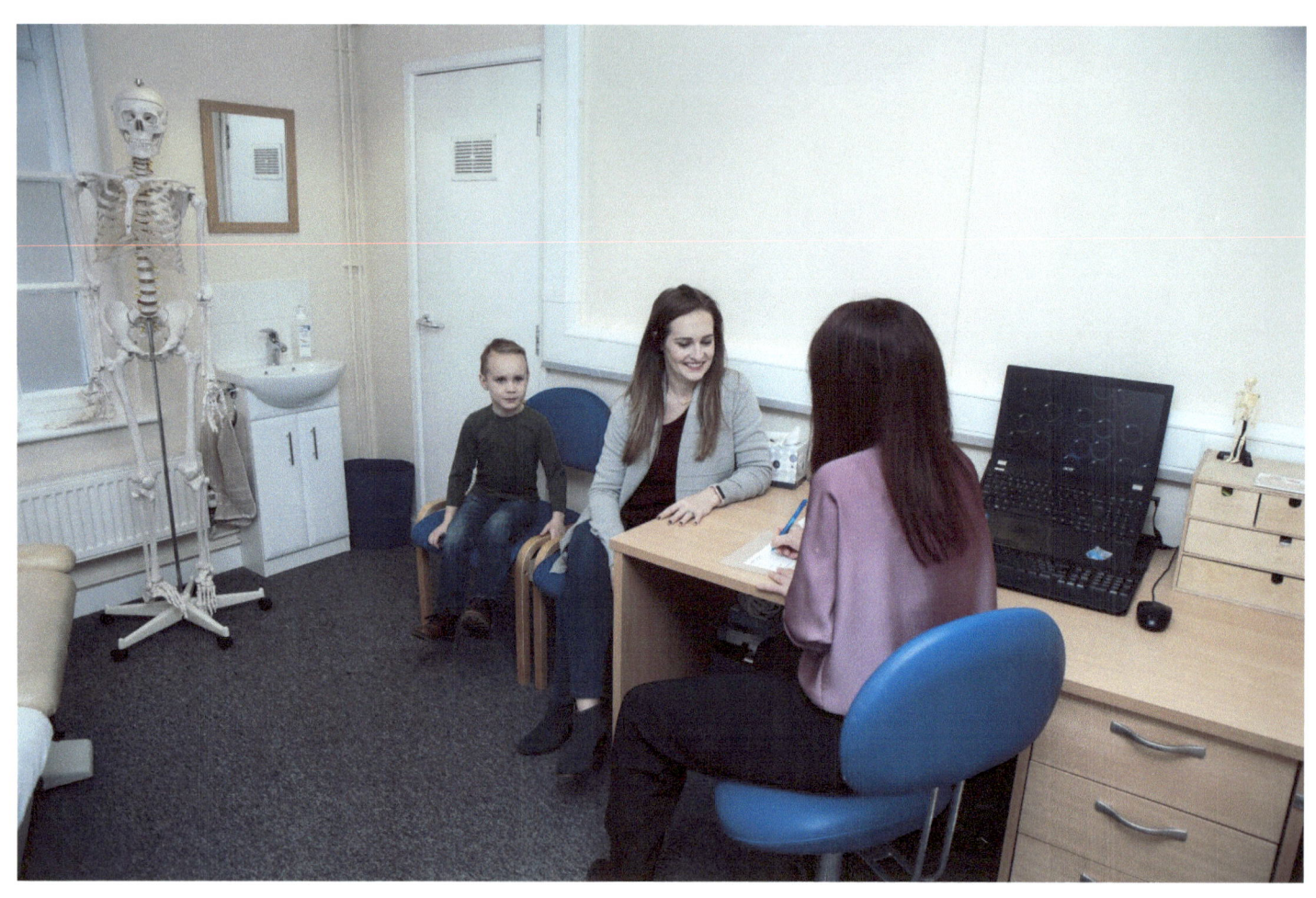

Mom schedules my next appointment.

We go home. Then I get to color my certificate.

Get your free bonus certificate and brochure.

Adults, go to:

www.courageouschiropractor.com/

Which book is your favorite?

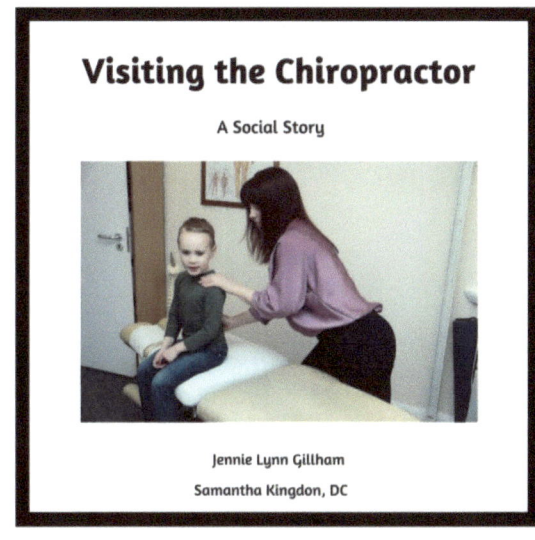
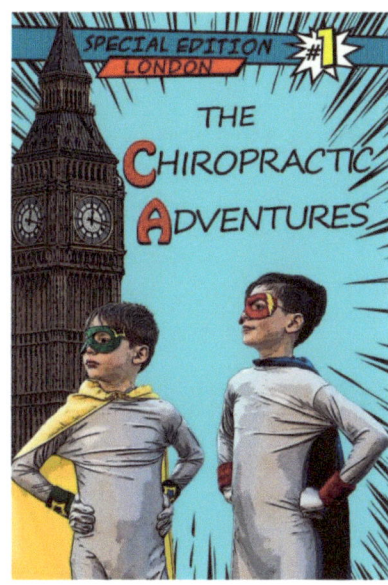

About the Authors

Samantha Kingdon is the co-author of *The Courageous Chiropractor and the Night Mare*. She is a chiropractor in Brandon, England whose patients include children, adults, and animals.

If she isn't seeing humans in the office or helping animals around town, you can find her lecturing at the UK location of Options for Animals.

Jennie Lynn Gillham is the creator of *The Courageous Chiropractor* series. In the books Freddy the fox and Lizzy the lizard face their fears and help injured animals.

Before becoming a full-time author and publisher, she was a ghostwriter specializing in memoirs. Her bachelor's degrees are in Media and Communications, and she has a master's degree in Creative Writing.

www.ingramcontent.com/pod-product-compliance
Lightning Source LLC
Chambersburg PA
CBHW041437010526
44118CB00002B/103